40 Intermediate
SNARE DRUM SOLOS
FOR CONCERT PERFORMANCE

In Australia Contact:
Hal Leonard Australia Pty. Ltd.
22 Taunton Drive, P.O. Box 5130
Cheltenham East, 3192 Victoria, Australia
Email:ausadmin@halleonard.com
ISBN 978-0-634-04912-5

HAL•LEONARD®
CORPORATION

7777 W. BLUEMOUND RD. P.O. BOX 13819 MILWAUKEE, WI 53213

About the Author

BEN HANS is a musician and music instructor in the greater Milwaukee area. He keeps a busy performance schedule throughout the upper Midwest, teaches music classes and percussion studies at Milwaukee Area Technical College, instructs more than sixty weekly private music students as well as the West Bend High School drum line, and serves as a consultant to many area school band programs. In addition to leading his own jazz trio, Ben performs regularly as a freelance artist.

An active member of the Percussive Arts Society, Ben holds an associate's degree in music from Milwaukee Area Technical College and a bachelor's degree in music from the University of Wisconsin. He is also the author of *Workin' Drums: 50 Solos for Drumset*, published by Hal Leonard Corporation.

AUTHOR'S NOTE: Any questions or comments regarding the music content of this book can be directed to the author via the Internet at www.benhans.com.

Dedication

This book is dedicated to two of my favorite percussionists, who have made the world a better place through their music making:

Vicki Jenks
Gifted teacher, mentor, and performer with the Wisconsin Chamber Orchestra... thank you.

Tito Puente
World famous bandleader, composer, and performer—an inspiration for many generations of percussionists to come. Farewell to the king; you are missed.

Contents

Preface

The demands on today's percussionists are greater than ever. *40 Intermediate Snare Drum Solos* is written to provide the maturing player with interesting solo material in many styles, as well as to assist in developing reading, musicianship, dynamic interpretation, and increased exposure to common rhythmic themes and meters.

This text can be used as a lesson supplement or as performance material for recital or solo competitions. A music glossary and Percussive Arts Society rudiment chart has been provided for reference.

- Remember: correct rhythmic articulation is important, so work up these solos slowly.
- Practice with a metronome, and in practice set the metronome 20-40 bpm slower than the indicated tempo marking.
- Follow dynamic markings. Correct dynamics will lead you to a very musical experience.
- Follow stickings throughout.

These solos are intended for concert snare performance, and should be played using concert snare stylings—i.e., with the closed (concert) roll and concert-style drags. However, today's percussionist needs to be aware of stylistic differences, and *some* of the material may also be *practiced* in parade or marching style (i.e., the double-stroke open roll). The help of an experienced teacher is always advisable.

It is my hope that the solos herein will provide fun and interesting practice ideas, increased knowledge of musical forms and terminology—as well as expose the developing player to new ideas within the multifaceted world of percussion music.

Good luck and good drumming.

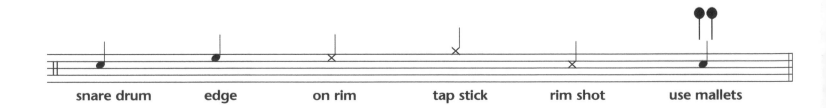

| snare drum | edge | on rim | tap stick | rim shot | use mallets |

Notation Legend

edge - edge of snare drum near rim

on rim - play on (counterhoop) rim of drum

tap stick - click sticks together at shoulder above drum

rim shot - strike drum so that stick strikes drumhead and rim simultaneously

use mallets - use medium or soft timpani mallet

Accent Etude in 2/4

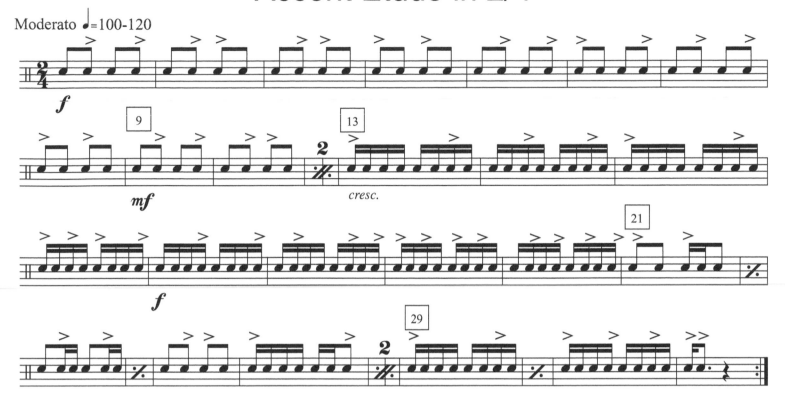

Accent Etude in 6/8

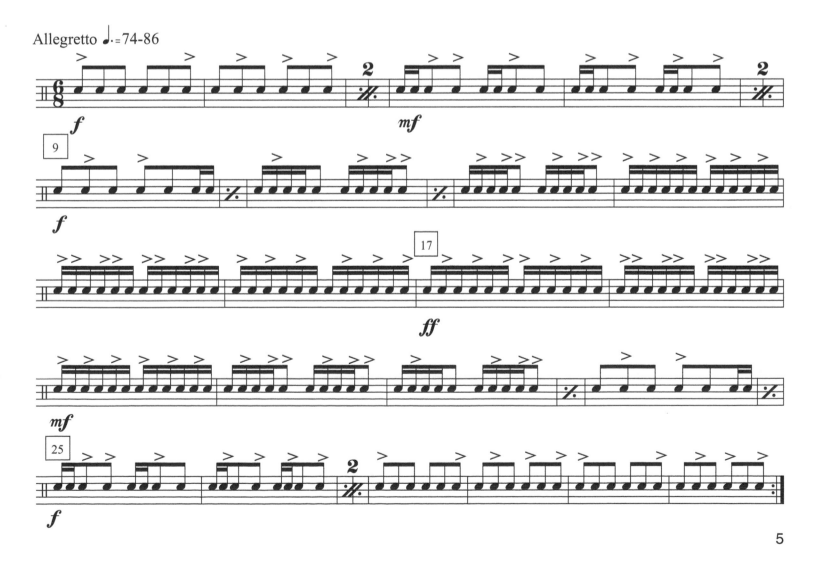

Adventure in Dynamics

A Time Perspective

The Whisper

Upstairs/Downstairs

Trio Grande

For Banes

Nine to Five

Five Friends

Meter Reader

Allegro ♪=172-196 (♪=♪ throughout)

February March

Friction

The Long and Short of It

Variations on a Tenor Drum Theme

The Wright Day at Kitty Hawk

Roll Up Your Sleeves

Moderato Vivace ♩= 108-120

On Target

Sam Lord's Castle

Moderato ♩.=58-62

Themes for Side Drum

The Waterfront

Flam Trap

The Mile

Moderato ♪=165-178 (♪ = ♪ throughout)

Split Decision

Replay

Moderato $\quad \bullet. = 52\text{-}58$

Tijuana Tap

Supra-Phonic Six-Eight

Dog 'n' Suds

The White House March

Sombrero Bolero

Gunslinger

Labyrinth

Allegretto con spirito ♪=148-160 (♪ = ♪ throughout)

Tools for the Trade

Allegretto ♩. = 42- 48

mf - mp

p

mf

f

ff

molto ritard.

sffz

36

Ol' Kent

Pearl Harbor Suite

Dedicated to the veterans of WWII Pacific Theatre

Mvt. I Prelude to a Storm

Mvt. II Day of Infamy

Mvt. III From Arizona to Missouri

Five Alarm Fire

El Diablo

Madcity Ramblin'

Dedicated to Vicki Jenks

Andante ♩=100

* Performance Note - m.25-30, Right hand near rim - piano. Left hand center of drum - mezzo forte.

For the King

In Memory of Tito Puente

* Performance Note - Rim strokes may be played on counterhoop *or* on side of drum to simulate timbale.

Stormcloud

Glossary
Music terms and articulations used in this book

Terms

accelerando	Gradually faster
alla marcia	In a march style
a tempo	Return to original tempo or rate of speed
con spirito	Joyfully, and with spirit
crescendo	⎯⎯⎯⎯⎯⎯ Gradually louder
decrescendo	⎯⎯⎯⎯⎯⎯ Gradually softer
diminuendo (dim.)	Becoming softer
Maestoso	Majestically
molto	Much, very
poco a poco	Little by little
ritardando	Gradually slower
sempre	Always, continually, throughout
simile	Continue in the same manner, style

Tempo Terms

Adagio	A slow movement
Andante	Moderately slow
Andantino	Less moderately, slightly faster than Andante
Allegretto	Moderately fast
Allegro	Quick, lively
Moderato	In moderate time
Prestissimo	Very fast time
Vivace	Lively, brisk, animated

Articulations

>	Accent	Play note with strong attack
∧	Marcato	Loud emphasized accent
·	Staccato	Short, detached
⌒·	Fermata	Hold out
//	Break (Railroad Tracks)	Short pause

Dynamics

ppp	Pianississimo	Very, very soft
pp	Pianissimo	Very soft
p	Piano	Soft
mp	Mezzo piano	Moderately soft
mf	Mezzo forte	Moderately loud
f	Forte	Loud
ff	Fortissimo	Very loud
fff	Fortississimo	Very very loud
sfz	Sforzando	Special stress and sudden emphasis
sffz	Sforzatiffimo	Perform with sudden emphasis at a very loud volume
fp	Forte piano	Loud, soft

Repeat terms and signs

D.C. (Da Capo)	Return to the beginning
D.S. (Dal Segno)	Return to the sign (𝄋)
Fine	End or close
𝄋	Section repeat sign
⊕	Coda sign, ending of an arrangement
D.C. al Fine	Da Capo, return to the beginning, play to fine
D.S. al Fine	Dal Segno, return to the sign (𝄋), play to fine
D.C. al Coda	Da Capo, return to the beginning, play to the coda sign (⊕), and skip to the coda
D.S. al Coda	Dal Segno, return to the sign (𝄋), play to the coda sign (⊕), skip to coda
play 4 times	Repeat as indicated

First ending (repeat, take second ending)

♩ = Metronome marking

2 ←Measure number

Neutral clef (percussion clef)

Bar Line

Music Staff

Repeat sign

Time Signature

Percussive Arts Society International Drum Rudiments

All rudiments should be practiced: open (slow) to close (fast) to open (slow)
and/or at an even moderate march tempo.

I. ROLL RUDIMENTS

A. Single Stroke Roll Rudiments

1. Single Stroke Roll*

R L R L R L R L

2. Single Stroke Four

R L R L   R L R L
L R L R   L R L R

3. Single Stroke Seven

R L R L R L R
L R L R L R L

B. Multiple Bounce Roll Rudiments

4. Multiple Bounce Roll

5. Triple Stroke Roll

R R R L L L R R R L L L

C. Double Stroke Open Roll Rudiments

6. Double Stroke Open Roll*

R R L L R R L L

7. Five Stroke Roll*

R   R L   L

8. Six Stroke Roll
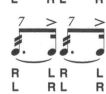
R   L R   L
L   R L   R

9. Seven Stroke Roll*

R   L R   L
L   R L   R

10. Nine Stroke Roll*
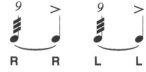
R   R   L   L

11. Ten Stroke Roll*

R   R L   R   R L

12. Eleven Stroke Roll*

R   R L   R   R L

13. Thirteen Stroke Roll*

R   R L   L

14. Fifteen Stroke Roll*

R   L R   L R
L   R L   R

15. Seventeen Stroke Roll
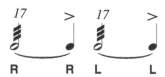
R   R   L   L

II. DIDDLE RUDIMENTS

16. Single Paradiddle*

R L R R L R L L

17. Double Paradiddle*

R L R L R R L R L R L L

18. Triple Paradiddle

R L R L R L R R L R L R L R L L

19. Single Paradiddle-Diddle

R L R R L L R L R R L L
L R L L R R L R L L R R

www.pas.org

III. FLAM RUDIMENTS

20. Flam*

LR   R L

22. Flam Accent*

LR L R RL R L

22. Flam Tap*

LR RrL LLR RrLL

23. Flamacue*

LR L R LLR
RL R L RrL

24. Flam Paradiddle*

LR L R RrL R LL

25. Single Flammed Mill

LR R L RrL L R L

26. Flam Paradiddle-
    Diddle*

LR L R RL LrL R L LRR

27. Pataflafla

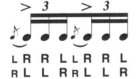

LR L R RrL LR L RrL

28. Swiss Army Triplet

LR R L LLR R L
RL L R RrL L R

29. Inverted Flam Tap

LR L RrL R LrL R LrL R

30. Flam Drag

LR L L LRrL R R L

IV. DRAG RUDIMENTS

31. Drag*

LLR   RRL

32. Single Drag Tap*

LLR L RrL R

33. Double Drag Tap*

LLRLLR L RrL RrL R

34. Lesson 25*

LLRL RLLRL R
RrL R L RrL R L

35. Single Dragadiddle

RRLR R LLRL L

36. Drag Paradiddle #1*

RLLR L RR LrrL R LL

37. Drag Paradiddle #2*

RLLRLLR L RRLrrL RrL RLL

38. Single Ratamacue*

LLRL RLRrL RLR

39. Double Ratamacue*

LLRLLRL RLRrL RrL RLR

40. Triple Ratamacue*

LLRLLRLLRLRLrrLrrLrrLRLR

For information on becoming a member of the Percussive Arts Society™ contact PAS® at:
701 N.W. Ferris Ave., Lawton, OK 73507 • (580) 353-1456 • E-mail: percarts@pas.org • Web site: www.pas.org

YOU CAN'T BEAT OUR DRUM BOOKS!

Bass Drum Control
Best Seller for More Than 50 Years!
by Colin Bailey
This perennial favorite among drummers helps players develop their bass drum technique and increase their flexibility through the mastery of exercises.
06620020 Book/Online Audio $17.99

The Complete Drumset Rudiments
by Peter Magadini
Use your imagination to incorporate these rudimental etudes into new patterns that you can apply to the drumset or tom toms as you develop your hand technique with the Snare Drum Rudiments, your hand and foot technique with the Drumset Rudiments and your polyrhythmic technique with the Polyrhythm Rudiments. Adopt them all into your own creative expressions based on ideas you come up with while practicing.
06620016 Book/CD Pack $14.95

Drum Aerobics
by Andy Ziker
A 52-week, one-exercise-per-day workout program for developing, improving, and maintaining drum technique. Players of all levels – beginners to advanced – will increase their speed, coordination, dexterity and accuracy. The online audio contains all 365 workout licks, plus play-along grooves in styles including rock, blues, jazz, heavy metal, reggae, funk, calypso, bossa nova, march, mambo, New Orleans 2nd Line, and lots more!
06620137 Book/Online Audio $19.99

Drumming the Easy Way!
The Beginner's Guide to Playing Drums for Students and Teachers
by Tom Hapke
Cherry Lane Music
Now with online audio! This book takes the beginning drummer through the paces – from reading simple exercises to playing great grooves and fills. Each lesson includes a preparatory exercise and a solo. Concepts and rhythms are introduced one at a time, so growth is natural and easy. Features large, clear musical print, intensive treatment of each individual drum figure, solos following each exercise to motivate students, and more!
02500876 Book/Online Audio...$19.99
02500191 Book...$14.99

The Drumset Musician – 2nd Edition
by Rod Morgenstein and Rick Mattingly
Containing hundreds of practical, usable beats and fills, *The Drumset Musician* teaches you how to apply a variety of patterns and grooves to the actual performance of songs. The accompanying online audio includes demos as well as 18 play-along tracks covering a wide range of rock, blues and pop styles, with detailed instructions on how to create exciting, solid drum parts.
00268369 Book/Online Audio...$19.99

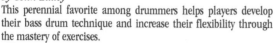

Instant Guide to Drum Grooves
The Essential Reference for the Working Drummer
by Maria Martinez
Become a more versatile drumset player! From traditional Dixieland to cutting-edge hip-hop, *Instant Guide to Drum Grooves* is a handy source featuring 100 patterns that will prepare working drummers for the stylistic variety of modern gigs. The book includes essential beats and grooves in such styles as: jazz, shuffle, country, rock, funk, New Orleans, reggae, calypso, Brazilian and Latin.
06620056 Book/CD Pack $12.99

1001 Drum Grooves
The Complete Resource for Every Drummer
by Steve Mansfield
Cherry Lane Music
This book presents 1,001 drumset beats played in a variety of musical styles, past and present. It's ideal for beginners seeking a well-organized, easy-to-follow encyclopedia of drum grooves, as well as consummate professionals who want to bring their knowledge of various drum styles to new heights. Author Steve Mansfield presents: rock and funk grooves, blues and jazz grooves, ethnic grooves, Afro-Cuban and Caribbean grooves, and much more.
02500337 Book..$14.99

Polyrhythms – The Musician's Guide
by Peter Magadini
edited by Wanda Sykes
Peter Magadini's *Polyrhythms* is acclaimed the world over and has been hailed by *Modern Drummer* magazine as "by far the best book on the subject." Written for instrumentalists and vocalists alike, this book with online audio contains excellent solos and exercises that feature polyrhythmic concepts. Topics covered include: 6 over 4, 5 over 4, 7 over 4, 3 over 4, 11 over 4, and other rhythmic ratios; combining various polyrhythms; polyrhythmic time signatures; and much more. The audio includes demos of the exercises and is accessed online using the unique code in each book.
06620053 Book/Online Audio..$19.99

Joe Porcaro's Drumset Method – Groovin' with Rudiments
Patterns Applied to Rock, Jazz & Latin Drumset
by Joe Porcaro
Master teacher Joe Porcaro presents rudiments at the drumset in this sensational new edition of *Groovin' with Rudiments*. This book is chock full of exciting drum grooves, sticking patterns, fills, polyrhythmic adaptations, odd meters, and fantastic solo ideas in jazz, rock, and Latin feels. The online audio features 99 audio clip examples in many styles to round out this true collection of superb drumming material for every serious drumset performer.
06620129 Book/Online Audio $24.99

66 Drum Solos for the Modern Drummer
Rock • Funk • Blues • Fusion • Jazz
by Tom Hapke
Cherry Lane Music
66 Drum Solos for the Modern Drummer presents drum solos in all styles of music in an easy-to-read format. These solos are designed to help improve your technique, independence, improvisational skills, and reading ability on the drums and at the same time provide you with some cool licks that you can use right away in your own playing.
02500319 Book/Online Audio..$17.99

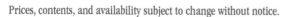
www.halleonard.com